seeworthybooks

read the fine print

P.O. Box 444
Washington Crossing, PA 18977
Published in the United States by Seeworthy Books, LLC
Printed in China

www.seeworthybooks.com

ISBN-10: 0-9830684-6-1
ISBN-13: 978-0-9830684-6-4

The Winter Night That Changed the World

☆ The Story of Washington's Crossing of the Delaware ☆

Written by Christine Carroll
Illustrated by Anthony Resto

A Message to Parents

My home is in Washington Crossing, Pennsylvania, about a mile from the spot where the Crossing took place.

My granddaughter Ava and I would often pass this site on our way home from her pre-school. When she was as little as 18 months old, I would tell her the story of Washington's famous crossing of the Delaware on Christmas night in 1776. Ava would clap her hands and ask me to tell her the story "da den" (again)!

My grandson Austin wanted to dress up like General Washington and begged for toy guns and swords so he could pretend he was a soldier in the Continental Army. The Crossing was so alive for Austin, he wanted to be a part of it!

Austin and I would often visit the gift shop at the Visitors Center in Washington Crossing. The books we found contained too much detail, and the vocabulary was far above the level of most preschoolers, kindergarteners and early grade school students. The Crossing story resonated with the little ones. That much I knew for sure. I also knew it needed to be retold in a way they could understand. And so the idea for The Winter Night That Changed the World was born.

Make the most of this "teachable moment," this opportunity to communicate important concepts like courage, commitment, leadership, patriotism and love of freedom...the ideals that made our country great... values that a child is never too young to learn.

Our responsibility as parents and as Americans is to ensure that every child knows the story of that cold, snowy Christmas night in 1776, the winter night that changed the world.

For Ava and Austin

America was once a group of thirteen
separate places called "colonies."
They were part of England and paid taxes
to the King whose name was George the Third.
The colonies wanted to form a country
of their own. They talked about calling it
The United States of America.

King George was angry when he heard this and sent soldiers to America to force the people to obey the laws of England.

The colonists decided to fight back.
Their leaders arranged a special meeting called
The Continental Congress.

They wrote "The Declaration of Independence," in which they told the whole world that America wanted to be free from England.

The Congress also got an army together. The soldiers fought long and hard against the English and lost many battles.

In the beginning of December, 1776, the Continental Army wound up at the Delaware River in Pennsylvania.

By Christmas, the soldiers were tired and hungry. Some had gotten hurt in the war, and some were sick from being cold and not having enough to eat. Some even ran away.

"Certainly independence isn't worth dying for," they said.

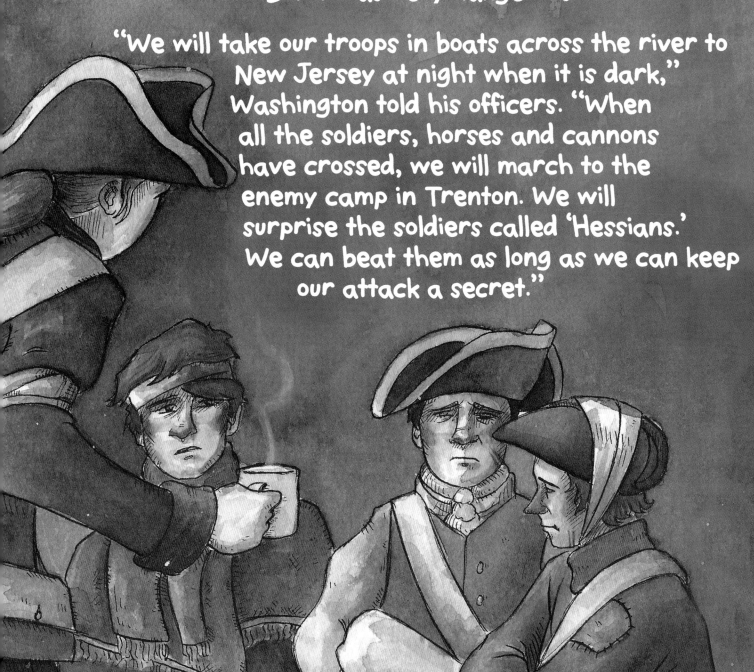

General Washington was a great leader. Instead of being discouraged and afraid, he came up with a plan. But it was very dangerous.

"We will take our troops in boats across the river to New Jersey at night when it is dark," Washington told his officers. "When all the soldiers, horses and cannons have crossed, we will march to the enemy camp in Trenton. We will surprise the soldiers called 'Hessians.' We can beat them as long as we can keep our attack a secret."

"Impossible!" some of the officers said. "How can we cross the river now? It is almost frozen over, and a snow storm is coming. Our men are hungry and some have no shoes or coats. They may not be able to make it. This is far too risky a plan."

General Washington was very brave. He convinced his officers they had no choice. He reminded them that their freedom was at stake. "Victory or death," he said.

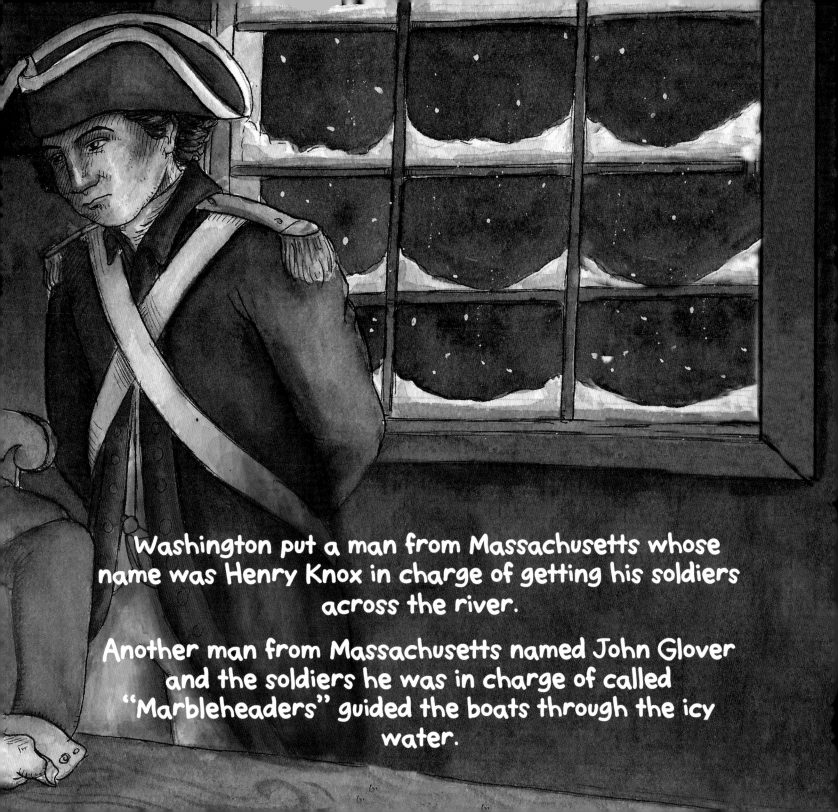

Washington put a man from Massachusetts whose name was Henry Knox in charge of getting his soldiers across the river.

Another man from Massachusetts named John Glover and the soldiers he was in charge of called "Marbleheaders" guided the boats through the icy water.

General Washington was in one of the first boats to cross the river. He wanted to show his men that he was not afraid. He was willing to risk his own life to prove that freedom for the colonies was worth fighting for.

The crossing took a long time. A few men fell in the water, but in the end, they all made it to the other side.

By that time it was almost morning. The officers told the soldiers they would have to walk about nine miles to Trenton to find the Hessians.

"But what about the surprise?" some of the soldiers said. "Daylight will be coming soon."

General Washington climbed on his horse and rode along beside his soldiers.
"Keep going men," he said. "Keep up with your officers."

The soldiers started the march to Trenton. They felt better as long as they could see General Washington.

He was their leader, and he was right there with them, telling them to be brave.

It was about 8 o'clock in the morning when the Continental Army got to Trenton.
A Hessian soldier spotted them and tried to warn his friends.

Suddenly Washington's men forgot how cold and tired they were. They followed General Washington and his officers. They used guns and cannons and swords against the Hessians.

After about an hour, the Hessians wanted to quit. Their leader, Johann Rall, tried to encourage his troops to fight on. When Rall got shot and fell off his horse, the soldiers decided to give up.

"We won. We won," the American troops cheered. Washington's plan had worked!

That same day the Continental Army had to go back
across the river to its camp in Pennsylvania.
The soldiers took their cannons and horses, and
now they had Hessian prisoners with them.
So the trip was even harder than before.

By now many of the men were exhausted. Their feet were bleeding, and their hands were numb from the cold.

But something was different.

The soldiers had started to believe in General Washington's words.

If they kept on fighting, maybe one day all thirteen colonies would come together.

They would become a real country called The United States of America, a place where people could live in peace and be free.

After the defeat of the Hessians at Trenton, the Continental Army started winning more battles. The war went on for a long time, and there were days when the soldiers felt tired and sad. But it was never the same as before.

They remembered the words their leader George Washington had said to them.

Freedom was worth any sacrifice they might have to make. Freedom was more important than anything.

The colonies finally won the war. No longer English "subjects," the people called themselves "citizens" of The United States of America.

They elected George Washington as their first
president. For that reason, and
because he was such a brave soldier and leader,
Washington is now called
"The Father of our Country."

Do you think George Washington and his soldiers could have ever imagined all the amazing things that would happen because of what they did so long ago?

America has become the greatest nation on earth, a land where people are free. Many thought this was impossible, but George Washington and his soldiers believed... on that dark, snowy night, December 25, 1776...the winter night that changed the world.

seeworthybooks

read the fine print

About The Author

Christine Carroll lives in Washington Crossing Pennsylvania, about a mile from the spot where the Crossing took place. The Carrolls' property is believed to have functioned as a mustering site for the Continental Army on the day of the Crossing. Ms. Carroll is a direct descendant of Michael Heaney who served in the 8th Pennsylvania Regiment during the Revolutionary War.

The Carroll Family owns and operates Crossing Vineyards and Winery in Washington Crossing, which they founded in 2000.

In addition to **The Winter Night That Changed the World**, Ms. Carroll has three children's books to her credit, as well as a novel, **Two Pennies Overboard**, which is set on Nantucket Island. A former high school English Teacher, Ms. Carroll holds Bachelor of Arts and Masters of Education degrees in English.

For more information visit her website: **www.seeworthybooks.com**.

About The Illustrator

Anthony Resto graduated from the American Academy of Art in Chicago with a BFA in watercolor and has been a children's book illustrator since 2009. His works include **One Nation Under God**, **Cold Whispers: Ghost at the Grand Inn**, and **Oracle of the Flying Badger**. You can view more of his work at **www.Anthonyresto.com**.

Afterword

No matter where you live, make it a point to visit
Washington Crossing Historic Park in Pennsylvania. A wonderful
Visitors Center has been built there and is a treasure trove of
information on the story of the Crossing. You can walk the river bank
where the Crossing actually happened. On Christmas day each year, a
re-enactment of the Crossing takes place. The experience is thrilling
and well worth postponing your turkey dinner for.
A portion of the proceeds of this book will be donated to The Friends
of Washington Crossing Park, a non-profit organization dedicated to
supporting and promoting the Park as a historic site.

Acknowledgements

My love and thanks to my husband Tom for his encouragement in the
creation of **The Winter Night That Changed The World.**
To Meg Sweeney, Chief Operating Officer of The David Library of the
American Revolution, thank you for being such a wonderful custodian
of this treasured repository of American history.
A special thanks to Larry Kidder, historian and retired teacher from
The Hun School in Princeton, New Jersey, whose knowledge and
passion for the Revolutionary period has helped me keep this story
grounded in fact.